The Path Of A Pilot: Daily Devotionals for Christian Pilots

Delightful Devotionals

CONTENTS

Introduction - Taking Off with Purpose and Faith

To the skilled aviators who navigate the boundless skies with precision and courage, this devotional is tailored for you—the guardians of the airspace, the seekers of the heavens. Within the cockpit, where altitude and attitude converge, and amidst the ceaseless hum of engines, this 21-day journey invites you to pause, reflect, and find spiritual connection.

Pilots, yours is a profession intertwined with the limitless wonders of flight, and in the beautiful expanse of the heavens, this devotional endeavors to be a companion on your airborne ventures. Each day unravels a new theme, drawing parallels between the challenges and triumphs of aviation and the timeless wisdom found in sacred scriptures.

From the call to trust in the flight plan to the pursuit of joy in service, from the embrace of diversity to the practice of gratitude, this devotional is crafted to resonate with the nuances of your unique journey.

As you ascend to new heights and navigate through the clouds, may these daily reflections serve as a source of inspiration, encouragement, and a reminder of the divine principles that guide your path.

Just as you command an aircraft through turbulence with skill and confidence, may this devotional offer a steadying influence, guiding you through the diverse landscapes of your professional and personal life.

Thank you for your dedication to the skies and the noble art of aviation. May this devotional be a companion, enriching your flights with purpose, resilience, and a deeper connection to the spiritual dimensions of your remarkable journey.

Day 1: Wings of Gratitude

Verse of the Day:

Psalm 103:2-5 - "Praise the LORD, my soul, and forget not all his benefits, who forgives all your sins and heals all your diseases, who redeems your life from the pit and crowns you with love and compassion."

Reflection:

In the vast expanse of the skies, as you embark on this devotional journey, let the wings of gratitude carry you. Today is an invitation to soar with a heart full of thanksgiving for the incredible gift of flight and the calling that has placed you among the clouds.

Embrace the joy that comes from recognizing the privilege of navigating the heavens, a privilege granted to you by a Creator who delights in granting us wings.

Take a moment to reflect on the countless blessings that come with being a pilot—the breathtaking views, the thrill of takeoff, and the sense of accomplishment with each safe landing.

Gratitude has the power to transform routine into a celebration and duty into a dance. As you navigate the boundless sky, let gratitude be the wind beneath your wings, propelling you forward with a spirit of appreciation.

Journal:

1. What specific aspects of your journey as a pilot are you most thankful for today?

2. How does expressing gratitude enhance your perspective on the responsibilities of flight?

3. In what ways can you share the joy of gratitude with your aviation community?

Prayer:

Heavenly Father, as I embark on this devotional journey, I am filled with gratitude for the incredible privilege of being a pilot. Thank you for the wings that carry me through the skies and the opportunities to navigate the wonders above. May my heart be continually attuned to the blessings of flight, and may my service in the air be an offering of thanksgiving to You. In Jesus' name, I pray. Amen.

Day 2: Trusting God's Flight Plan

Verse of the Day:

Proverbs 3:5-6 - "Trust in the LORD with all your heart and lean not on your own understanding; in all your ways submit to him, and he will make your paths straight."

Reflection:

In the cockpit of life, trust becomes the compass that guides your journey through the clouds and uncertainties. Today, I encourage you to surrender the controls of your heart to the divine Pilot who charts the course of your life.

As a pilot, you understand the importance of trust in your instruments, and similarly, placing your trust in God's flight plan brings a profound sense of peace and assurance. Consider the profound truth embedded in Proverbs 3:5-6: "Trust in the LORD with all your heart and lean not on your own understanding; in all your ways submit to him, and he will make your paths straight."

Just as you rely on navigational instruments for a smooth flight, your trust in God becomes the stabilizing force that aligns your journey with His divine purpose.

Journal:

1. Reflect on a time when trusting in God's plan brought clarity and direction to a challenging situation.

2. How can your trust in God positively influence your decision-making both in the cockpit and in daily life?

3. In what ways can you deepen your trust in God as the ultimate Navigator of your life's journey?

Prayer:

Heavenly Father, today I choose to trust in Your flight plan for my life. Just as I rely on instruments for navigation, I surrender my heart to Your divine guidance. Help me trust in You with all aspects of my journey, both in the air and on the ground. May Your presence be the stabilizing force that aligns my path with Your purpose. In Your trustworthy name, I pray. Amen.

Day 3: Fellowship at Altitude

Verse of the Day:

Ecclesiastes 4:12 - "Though one may be overpowered, two can defend themselves. A cord of three strands is not quickly broken."

Reflection:

As a pilot, you understand the significance of teamwork and collaboration in the cockpit. Today, let's explore the parallel truth of fellowship in your personal and professional life.

Ecclesiastes 4:12 reminds us, "Though one may be overpowered, two can defend themselves. A cord of three strands is not quickly broken." In the sky and in life, the bonds of fellowship strengthen us, providing support during challenges and adding richness to our experiences.

Consider the relationships you've built within the aviation community—fellow pilots, air traffic controllers, and the broader aviation family.

These connections are not just professional; they're threads of support that weave through the fabric of your journey. Today, take a moment to appreciate the camaraderie and unity that fellowship brings, recognizing the collective strength it provides.

Journal:

1. Reflect on a time when collaboration or teamwork significantly enhanced a flying experience.

2. How can you contribute to fostering a sense of fellowship within the aviation community?

3. Consider the different "strands" in your support network. How do these relationships contribute to your overall strength?

Prayer:

Dear Lord, I thank You for the gift of fellowship in both my professional and personal life. Help me appreciate the strength found in unity and collaboration. May I be a source of support for others and find strength in the bonds of fellowship. Bless the aviation community with a spirit of unity and shared purpose. In Jesus' name, I pray. Amen.

Day 4: Precision in Faithful Service

Verse of the Day:

Colossians 3:23 - "Whatever you do, work at it with all your heart, as working for the Lord, not for human masters."

Reflection:

In the precision of flight, there is a reflection of the meticulous care with which we are called to serve. Colossians 3:23 guides us: "Whatever you do, work at it with all your heart, as working for the Lord, not for human masters."

Today, let's delve into the connection between the precision required in piloting and the faithful service we are called to offer in every aspect of our lives.

As a pilot, you know that precision is not just about accuracy but also about dedication and commitment.

Every adjustment, every decision, and every action is made with careful consideration. Likewise, in our service to others, especially in the noble role of a pilot, precision becomes a form of worship—a way to honor the responsibilities entrusted to us.

Journal:

1. How does the precision required in piloting translate into the quality of service you provide to passengers and colleagues?

2. In what ways can you infuse your daily tasks, both in the cockpit and beyond, with a sense of precision and dedication?

3. Reflect on a moment when your commitment to precision positively impacted the outcome of a situation.

Prayer:

Heavenly Father, as I navigate the skies and serve in various capacities, help me approach each task with the precision and dedication it deserves. May my actions reflect a heart devoted to faithful service, honoring You in all that I do. Guide me to embrace the call to excellence in every aspect of my life. In Your name, I pray. Amen.

Day 5: Calm Amidst the Turbulence

Verse of the Day:

Isaiah 41:10 - "So do not fear, for I am with you; do not be dismayed, for I am your God. I will strengthen you and help you; I will uphold you with my righteous right hand."

Reflection:

In the ever-changing skies, turbulence is inevitable, both in flight and in life. Today, let's draw inspiration from Isaiah 41:10, "So do not fear, for I am with you; do not be dismayed, for I am your God. I will strengthen you and help you; I will uphold you with my righteous right hand."

As a pilot, you understand the importance of remaining calm in the face of turbulence, and similarly, in life, God offers a source of unwavering strength and peace. Take a moment to reflect on the challenges you've faced, both in the cockpit and beyond.

Consider the times when you found inner strength and calmness, realizing that God's presence is a stabilizing force even in the midst of life's storms. Today, embrace the reassurance that comes from knowing that you are not alone, and that God's righteous hand upholds you.

Journal:

1. Recall a situation where remaining calm proved essential, either in flight or in daily life. How did you navigate through it?

2. How can the knowledge of God's constant presence bring calmness to your heart during challenging times?

3. In what ways can you share the peace you find in God with those around you?

Prayer:

Dear Lord, as I encounter turbulence in the skies and the challenges of life, I seek Your calming presence. Thank you for being my source of strength and peace. Help me navigate through difficulties with faith, knowing that Your righteous hand upholds me. May Your peace reign in my heart and overflow into the lives of those I encounter. In Your comforting name, I pray. Amen.

Day 6: Navigating Life's Flight Plan

Verse of the Day:

Psalm 119:105 - "Your word is a lamp for my feet, a light on my path."

Reflection:

Just as a pilot carefully plans and navigates each flight, our lives are on a journey with a unique flight plan designed by our Creator.

Today, let's reflect on Psalm 119:105, "Your word is a lamp for my feet, a light on my path." In the cockpit, instruments guide you through the skies, and similarly, God's Word serves as a guiding light for our journey through life. Consider the various decisions and crossroads you encounter, both in aviation and personal choices.

How does God's Word illuminate your path and provide guidance? Today, embrace the truth that, just like a well-charted flight plan, God's Word offers wisdom and direction for every step of your life's journey.

Journal:

1. Reflect on a time when guidance from God's Word influenced a significant decision in your life.

2. In what ways can you intentionally incorporate God's guidance into your daily routines, both personally and professionally?

3. Consider the parallels between navigating a flight plan and following the guidance of God's Word. How can these principles be applied in unison?

Prayer:

Heavenly Father, I thank You for the guidance Your Word provides in every aspect of my life. As I navigate through the skies and the journey of life, may Your Word be a lamp to my feet and a light on my path. Help me seek Your wisdom in all decisions, trusting that Your guidance leads to a purposeful and fulfilling journey. In Jesus' name, I pray. Amen.

Day 7: Safety in God's Wings

Verse of the Day:

Psalm 91:4 - "He will cover you with his feathers, and under his wings you will find refuge; his faithfulness will be your shield and rampart."

Reflection:

Amidst the vastness of the skies, safety is paramount. Reflect on Psalm 91:4, "He will cover you with his feathers, and under his wings you will find refuge; his faithfulness will be your shield and rampart."

Just as a pilot ensures the safety of passengers in flight, our ultimate safety rests under the protective wings of our Creator. Consider the times when you've experienced a sense of refuge, whether during challenging flights or in the uncertainties of life.

Today, embrace the truth that God's faithfulness is a shield that guards and a rampart that provides security. As you navigate the skies and the complexities of life, find comfort in the safety found under God's wings.

Journal:

1. Recall a moment when you felt a sense of refuge and safety, either in the cockpit or in life. How did this impact your perspective?

2. How can the awareness of God's protective wings influence your approach to challenges and uncertainties?

3. Consider ways to share the concept of divine refuge with others, both within and beyond the aviation community.

Prayer:

Dear Lord, I find safety and refuge under Your wings. In the skies and in life, I trust in Your faithfulness as a shield and rampart. Thank you for being my ultimate source of security. Guide me to extend this sense of refuge to others and to live with confidence in Your protective care. In Jesus' name, I pray. Amen.

Day 8: Beyond Boundaries: God's Global Mission

Verse of the Day:

Matthew 28:19-20 - "Therefore go and make disciples of all nations, baptizing them in the name of the Father and of the Son and of the Holy Spirit."

Reflection:

As a pilot, your journey transcends borders, and today, let's explore the broader mission outlined in Matthew 28:19-20, "Therefore go and make disciples of all nations, baptizing them in the name of the Father and of the Son and of the Holy Spirit."

Reflect on the global impact of your role and how it aligns with the greater mission God sets before us. Consider the diversity encountered in your aviation experiences and the opportunities for connection and influence. Today, embrace the idea that your journey is part of a broader mission—a call to impact the world beyond geographical boundaries.

As you navigate the skies, recognize the potential to bring the message of hope and purpose to people from all walks of life.

Journal:

1. How have your aviation experiences allowed you to connect with individuals from diverse backgrounds?

2. In what ways can you integrate the global mission outlined in Matthew 28:19-20 into your daily interactions within the aviation community?

3. Reflect on the impact your journey can have on a broader scale. What steps can you take to make a positive difference in the lives of those you encounter?

Prayer:

Heavenly Father, as I embark on this global mission through aviation, guide me to be a beacon of hope and purpose. Help me connect with individuals from diverse backgrounds, sharing Your love and truth along the way. May my journey contribute to the broader mission of making disciples of all nations. In Jesus' name, I pray. Amen.

Day 9: The Navigator's Rest: Trusting God's Timing

Verse of the day:

Ecclesiastes 3:1 - "There is a time for everything, and a season for every activity under the heavens."

Reflection:

In the fast-paced world of aviation, waiting for the right conditions is crucial. Ecclesiastes 3:1 reminds us, "There is a time for everything, and a season for every activity under the heavens."

Today, let's explore the concept of waiting patiently and trusting God's perfect timing in our lives. Consider the moments of waiting you've experienced in aviation, whether for clear skies, favorable winds, or safe conditions. Reflect on how this parallels the waiting seasons in life.

Today, embrace the truth that just as a pilot must wait for optimal conditions, we, too, must trust God's timing in every aspect of our journey.

Journal:

1. Recall a time when waiting patiently led to a positive outcome, either in aviation or personal life.

2. How can the understanding of Ecclesiastes 3:1 influence your perspective on waiting for God's timing?

3. Consider areas in your life where patience and trust in God's timing are needed. What steps can you take to wait faithfully?

Prayer:

Dear Lord, teach me the art of waiting patiently and trusting Your perfect timing. In the skies and in life, help me understand that there is a season for every activity under the heavens. Grant me the patience to wait faithfully for Your guidance and the assurance that Your timing is always perfect. In Your Holy name, I pray. Amen.

Day 10: Altitude of Gratitude: Recognizing God's Provision

Verse of the Day:

Philippians 4:19 - "And my God will meet all your needs according to the riches of his glory in Christ Jesus."

Reflection:

In the altitude of flight, we witness the vastness of God's creation. Today, let's explore the connection between gratitude and recognizing God's provision, drawing inspiration from Philippians 4:19, "And my God will meet all your needs according to the riches of his glory in Christ Jesus."

Consider the moments of provision and abundance you've experienced in your aviation journey. Reflect on how these instances parallel God's provision in your personal life.

Today, embrace a heart of gratitude, recognizing that God's abundant provision extends beyond the cockpit into every facet of your existence.

Journal:

1. Reflect on a specific moment in your aviation career when you experienced God's provision.

2. How can the awareness of God's provision influence your daily perspective and interactions within the aviation community?

3. Consider areas in your life where gratitude can be deepened. What specific steps can you take to cultivate a heart of gratitude?

Prayer:

Heavenly Father, I am grateful for Your abundant provision in every aspect of my life, both in the skies and on the ground. Help me recognize and appreciate Your constant care and generosity. May a heart of gratitude shape my interactions and attitudes within the aviation community and beyond. In Jesus' name, I pray. Amen.

Day 11: Clear Skies of Wisdom: Seeking God's Guidance

Verse of the Day:

James 1:5 - "If any of you lacks wisdom, you should ask God, who gives generously to all without finding fault, and it will be given to you."

Reflection:

Just as a pilot navigates through various weather conditions, seeking wisdom is essential for navigating the complexities of life.

James 1:5 offers a guiding principle: "If any of you lacks wisdom, you should ask God, who gives generously to all without finding fault, and it will be given to you."

Reflect on the significance of seeking God's wisdom in your aviation decisions and in the broader aspects of your life. Today, embrace the truth that, like a skilled pilot relying on instruments, seeking God's wisdom provides clarity and direction for every decision and journey.

Journal:

1. Recall a time when seeking God's wisdom played a crucial role in a decision you made.

2. How can the pursuit of wisdom impact your interactions within the aviation community and contribute to a culture of learning?

3. Consider areas in your life where you need wisdom. What steps can you take to intentionally seek God's guidance?

Prayer:

Dear Lord, I seek Your wisdom in every decision, both in the skies and in life. Grant me discernment and clarity as I navigate through challenges. Help me foster a culture of learning within the aviation community, and may seeking Your wisdom be a continuous journey. In Jesus' name, I pray. Amen.

Day 12: The Compass of Compassion: Extending God's Love

Verse of the Day:

Colossians 3:12 - "Therefore, as God's chosen people, holy and dearly loved, clothe yourselves with compassion, kindness, humility, gentleness and patience."

Reflection:

Just as you use a compass for navigation in flight, compassion serves as a guiding force in our interactions with others. Colossians 3:12 encourages us, "Therefore, as God's chosen people, holy and dearly loved, clothe yourselves with compassion, kindness, humility, gentleness and patience."

Reflect on the role of compassion in your aviation experiences and consider how it can shape your interactions within the aviation community and beyond.

Today, embrace the truth that, like a compass pointing north, compassion directs our actions and responses toward reflecting God's love.

Journal:

1. Recall a situation where compassion played a significant role in your aviation interactions.

2. How can you intentionally cultivate a spirit of compassion within the aviation community, fostering a supportive and empathetic culture?

3. Consider areas in your life where you can extend God's love through acts of compassion. What steps can you take to incorporate compassion into your daily interactions?

Prayer:

Heavenly Father, I am grateful for Your compassion, and I pray that it may guide my interactions with others. Clothe me with compassion, kindness, humility, gentleness, and patience, reflecting Your love in the aviation community and beyond. May my actions be a testament to Your grace. In Jesus' name, I pray. Amen.

Day 13: Wings of Perseverance: Facing Challenges with Faith

Verse of the Day:

Psalm 31:24 - "Be strong and take heart, all you who hope in the LORD."

Reflection:

Just as you persevere through challenges in every flight, the journey of life often demands unwavering perseverance. Psalm 31:24 encourages us, "Be strong and take heart, all you who hope in the LORD."

Today, let's explore the connection between perseverance and faith, drawing inspiration from the challenges you've faced in the skies. Reflect on instances where perseverance played a crucial role in overcoming difficulties. Consider how faith, much like a steady hand on the controls, provides strength during challenging times.

Choose to embrace the truth that, just as you navigate through turbulence with resolve, faith empowers you to face life's challenges with a heart full of hope.

Journal

1. Recall a specific challenge you've faced in your aviation career and reflect on how perseverance and faith played a role in overcoming it.

2. How can the understanding of Psalm 31:24 guide your perspective when encountering challenges, both in the cockpit and in life?

3. Consider areas in your life where perseverance is needed. What steps can you take to strengthen your resolve and face challenges with faith?

Prayer:

Dear Lord, grant me the strength to persevere through challenges, both in the skies and on the ground. May my hope in You be a source of courage and resilience. Guide me through difficulties, and let faith be the steady hand that navigates me through life's turbulence. In Your empowering name, I pray. Amen.

Day 14: Harmony in the Skies: Balancing Responsibilities

Verse of the Day:

Micah 6:8 - "He has shown you, O mortal, what is good. And what does the LORD require of you? To act justly and to love mercy and to walk humbly with your God."

Reflection:

In the vast expanse of the skies, balance is essential for a harmonious flight. Micah 6:8 provides a guiding principle: "He has shown you, O mortal, what is good. And what does the LORD require of you? To act justly and to love mercy and to walk humbly with your God."

Today, let's explore the concept of balance in our responsibilities, both as pilots and individuals. Reflect on how the pursuit of justice, mercy, and humility plays a role in your aviation experiences and personal life.

Embrace the truth that, like a well-balanced aircraft, our lives find harmony when we align ourselves with God's principles of justice, mercy, and humility.

Journal:

1. Consider how the principles of Micah 6:8 can be applied in your aviation career and personal life.

2. How can you actively seek justice, love mercy, and walk humbly in your interactions within the aviation community?

3. Reflect on instances where finding a balance between responsibilities led to positive outcomes. What lessons can you draw from those experiences?

Prayer:

Heavenly Father, guide me in seeking a balance in my responsibilities, both in the skies and in life. Help me act justly, love mercy, and walk humbly with You. May my life reflect the harmony that comes from aligning with Your principles. In Jesus' name, I pray. Amen.

Day 15: Radiant Presence: Shining God's Light

Verse of the Day:

Matthew 5:16 -"In the same way, let your light shine before others, that they may see your good deeds and glorify your Father in heaven."

Reflection:

In the vast openness of the skies, light breaks through the darkness. Matthew 5:16 guides us, "In the same way, let your light shine before others, that they may see your good deeds and glorify your Father in heaven."

Today, let's explore the idea of shining God's light in the aviation community and beyond. Reflect on how your actions, both in the cockpit and in personal interactions, can be a source of light for others.

Consider the impact of positive deeds on those around you. Choose to embrace the truth that, like a beacon in the night, your radiant presence has the power to glorify God and inspire those you encounter.

Journal:

1. Recall a moment when you experienced the positive impact of someone else's radiant presence. How did it influence you?

2. How can you intentionally let your light shine within the aviation community, bringing positivity and encouragement to others?

3. Consider areas in your life where you can be a source of light. What specific actions can you take to glorify God through your deeds?

Prayer:

Dear Lord, may my life be a radiant presence, reflecting Your light in the aviation community and beyond. Guide me to let my light shine through positive deeds, bringing glory to Your name. May my actions inspire others and point them towards You. In Your Holy name, I pray. Amen.

Day 16: Divine Coordinates: Aligning with God's Will

Verse of the Day:

Proverbs 3:6 - "In all your ways acknowledge him, and he will make straight your paths."

Reflection:

Proverbs 3:6 offers a profound directive for our life's journey, likening it to a divine coordination with God's will.

The imagery of aligning our ways with His acknowledges the significance of seeking God's guidance in every aspect of our lives. This divine coordination assures us that when we acknowledge God in all our endeavors, our paths become straightened by His wisdom and purpose.

Just as precise coordinates guide us through the skies, aligning with God's will provides us with clarity and assurance in navigating the complexities of life.

As we reflect on this scripture, consider the areas of your life where you have acknowledged God's presence and sought His guidance. How has aligning with God's will influenced the direction of your paths?

Journal:

1. Reflect on a specific instance when acknowledging God in your decisions led to a clear and purposeful path.

2. Are there areas in your life where you have struggled to align with God's will? What steps can you take to enhance this alignment?

3. In what ways can you encourage others to acknowledge God in their journeys, fostering a community aligned with divine coordinates?

Prayer:

Heavenly Father, as we journey through life, we seek Your divine coordinates to align our paths with Your will. Grant us the wisdom to acknowledge You in all our ways, trusting that in doing so, our paths will be made straight. Guide us through the complexities of life, and may our hearts be attuned to Your divine coordination. Strengthen our commitment to seek Your guidance in every aspect of our journey. In Your holy name, we pray. Amen.

Day 17: God's Comfort in Difficult Times

Verse of the Day:

Psalm 34:18 - "The LORD is near to the brokenhearted and saves the crushed in spirit."

Reflection:

In the midst of life's storms, Psalm 34:18 paints a comforting image of God's proximity to those facing brokenness and despair. Like clouds that envelop the sky, His presence surrounds and embraces the brokenhearted.

This scripture assures us that God not only draws near to us in times of difficulty but also saves those whose spirits are crushed. Just as clouds bring rain to nurture the earth, God's comfort showers upon us, providing solace and renewal in our times of deepest need.

In the cloudy moments of life, His closeness becomes a source of encouragement and restoration.

Journal:

1. Reflect on a time when you felt the nearness of God during a difficult season. How did His presence bring comfort and strength?

2. Are there individuals in your life currently facing brokenness or despair? How can you be a source of God's comfort to them?

3. Consider the metaphor of clouds bringing rain for nourishment. How might God's comfort bring renewal and growth in challenging times?

Prayer:

Heavenly Father, we find solace in the assurance that You are near to the brokenhearted and that You save the crushed in spirit. In difficult times, envelop us in the comforting clouds of Your presence. May Your nearness bring renewal and strength, especially to those experiencing brokenness. Empower us to be vessels of Your comfort, sharing Your love with those in need. In Jesus' name, we pray. Amen.

Day 18: Steadfast Anchors: Grounded in God's Promises

Verse of the Day:

2 Corinthians 1:20 - "For all the promises of God find their Yes in him. That is why it is through him that we utter our Amen to God for his glory."

Reflection:

In the turbulence of life's challenges, we find solace and strength in God's unwavering promises. 2 Corinthians 1:20 reassures us that every promise of God is fulfilled in Christ, providing a steadfast anchor for our faith.

Like an aircraft tethered securely to the ground, our lives are anchored in the promises of God. This scripture encourages us to declare our "Amen" in acknowledgment of His faithfulness and to ground ourselves in the unshakeable certainty of His Word.

As we face the uncertainties of life, these promises become our steadfast anchors, keeping us firm in our faith journey.

Journal:

1. Reflect on a promise of God that has been an anchor in challenging times. How did it provide stability and reassurance?

2. Are there areas in your life where you need to trust more in God's promises? How can you deepen your reliance on His unchanging Word?

3. Consider sharing a promise of God with someone facing difficulties. How might the assurance of His promises impact their perspective?

Prayer:

Heavenly Father, we anchor our lives in the unshakeable promises found in Your Word. As we face life's uncertainties, may Your promises be our steadfast anchors, providing stability and reassurance. Help us to declare our "Amen" in faith, acknowledging Your faithfulness in every season. Grant us the strength to trust more in Your promises and to share the assurance of Your Word with those in need. In Jesus' name, we pray. Amen.

Day 19: Heavenly Resilience: Overcoming Adversity with Faith

Verse of the Day:

James 1:12 - "Blessed is the one who perseveres under trial because, having stood the test, that person will receive the crown of life that the Lord has promised to those who love him."

Reflection:

James 1:12 illuminates the path of heavenly resilience, assuring us that those who endure trials with faith receive a promised crown of life. The imagery of standing the test reflects the strength that adversity builds within us, akin to the refining process that shapes precious metals.

In times of trial, our faith becomes a resilient force, helping us overcome challenges and leading us toward the promised reward of eternal life. This scripture calls us to view adversity not as an obstacle but as an opportunity for our faith to grow and for God's promises to unfold.

Journal:

1. Reflect on a challenging time in your life when perseverance strengthened your faith. How did you experience God's presence in the midst of adversity?

2. How can you view current challenges as opportunities for spiritual growth and resilience? What aspects of your faith need strengthening during difficult times?

3. Consider the concept of the "crown of life." How does the promise of eternal life impact your perspective on enduring trials with faith?

4.

Prayer:

Gracious Lord, we find strength in Your promise that blessed are those who persevere under trial. Help us view adversity through the lens of heavenly resilience, knowing that our faith is refined in the fires of life's challenges. Grant us the perseverance to stand the test and the assurance of the crown of life promised to those who love You. In Your name, we pray. Amen.

Day 20: Adapting to God's Transformative Power

Verse of the Day:

Romans 12:2 - "Do not conform to the pattern of this world, but be transformed by the renewing of your mind. Then you will be able to test and approve what God's will is—his good, pleasing and perfect will."

Reflection:

In the vast expanse of the skies, pilots encounter a symphony of changes and challenges, much like the ever-shifting patterns of the world.

Romans 12:2 beckons us, especially as pilots, to transcend mere conformity and embrace a continual renewal—a spiritual recalibration akin to the meticulous checks performed on our aircraft. Adapting to the transformative power of God is not just a suggestion but a necessity for those who navigate the boundless heavens.

It's the art of adjusting our mental course, much like we adjust our flight path to the winds aloft.

This scripture becomes our compass, guiding us through the intricacies of our profession, ensuring our minds are attuned to God's perfect will, like instruments finely tuned for optimal performance.

Journal:

1. Recall a moment in your aviation career when the winds of change required a significant adjustment. How did a renewed mindset impact your decision-making and overall experience?

2. In the dynamic field of aviation, how can the transformative power of God enhance your ability to discern His will amidst the complexities of the industry?

3. Ponder on the parallels between adjusting to changing winds during flight and adapting to life's shifts. How can you navigate the winds of change in your professional life with a mindset open to God's transformative guidance?

4.

Prayer:

Heavenly Father, as pilots navigating the skies, we seek Your guidance not merely to conform but to be continually transformed by the renewing of our minds. In the fluid landscape of aviation, help us adapt to the winds of change with a renewed mindset, attuned to Your perfect will. Grant us the wisdom to navigate the complexities of our profession while staying true to Your purpose. In Jesus' name, we pray. Amen.

Day 21: Heavenly Celebration: Reflecting God's Glory

Verse of the Day:

1 Corinthians 10:31 - "So whether you eat or drink or whatever you do, do it all for the glory of God."

Reflection:

As you conclude this devotional journey, 1 Corinthians 10:31 serves as a resounding anthem echoing through the heavenly realm. In the daily intricacies of our lives, whether soaring through the skies or grounded on earthly tasks, this scripture becomes a compass guiding our actions.

Every pre-flight check, each communication, and even the simplest acts become opportunities to reflect God's glory. It's a call to celebrate the heavenly symphony of our profession, ensuring that every maneuver, every decision, resonates with the harmonies of God's purpose.

Just as the sun sets, casting hues of brilliance across the heavens, may our lives, both in the cockpit and beyond, radiate God's glory.

Journal:

1. Reflect on your aviation journey. In what ways have you consciously sought to bring glory to God in your daily tasks and interactions within the aviation community?

2. As you consider 1 Corinthians 10:31, how can you further integrate the principle of doing everything for the glory of God into your professional and personal life?

3. In the realm of aviation, what intentional steps can you take to reflect God's glory to those around you, be it fellow pilots, air traffic controllers, or passengers?

Prayer:

Gracious Lord, as we conclude this devotional journey, we are reminded to do everything for Your glory. In our aviation endeavors and in the daily tapestry of our lives, may our actions be a heavenly celebration reflecting Your splendor. Guide us to navigate the skies and the ground with a profound awareness of Your presence, ensuring that every aspect of our journey glorifies You. In Your Holy name, we pray. Amen.

Conclusion: Landing with Gratitude and Hope

As we conclude this 21-day devotional journey, imagine your aircraft gracefully descending, marking the end of a flight. In a similar manner, this devotional bids farewell with gratitude and hope, acknowledging the profound journey shared between faith and flight.

To the pilots who have embraced each daily reflection, thank you for allowing these moments of pause and reflection into your cockpit. As you land with the aircraft's wheels meeting the runway, may you also land with a heart filled with gratitude—for the challenges faced, the victories achieved, and the unwavering presence of faith that guided you.

In aviation, every landing is a testament to skill, preparation, and teamwork. Similarly, may the insights gained from these devotionals be a testament to your spiritual preparation, resilience, and the support you find in the greater aviation community.

As you disembark from this devotional journey, carry the hope instilled by the promises of scripture into the next leg of your life's flight.

Just as you prepare for the next takeoff, may you also prepare to face each day with the enduring principles of faith, purpose, and the unwavering belief that, like a well-executed landing, each conclusion is a precursor to a new beginning.

Thank you for entrusting your moments of reflection to this devotional. May your flights be safe, your journeys be filled with purpose, and may the hope found in faith continue to guide you through the skies of life.

Until we embark on the next spiritual journey together, land with gratitude, and may your days ahead be blessed with endless horizons and clear skies. Safe travels, and may your faith-infused journey continue to soar to new heights.

With warmest wishes and gratitude,

Delightful Devotionals